AF322693

SISTER BLUES TERRIBLE TWOS

WRITTEN BY : DR.TIRRELL WOODSON

ILLUSTRATED BY : SHAHZAIB

Dedicated to

My wife, a wonderful mother, and my three daughters, Zaria, Zalia, and Za'hara. All these beautiful ladies inspire me daily.

In a cozy house, there were two
happy twins, aged five. They
had a little sister named Zo,
who was just two, and a loving Mom.

The twins were always full of energy, and Zo was always excited. Their Mom was kind and took care of them all. Baby Zo was full of energy, ready to kick and shout at any time of day. Her adorable smile could melt hearts, but it was also her secret weapon to get her way. "I mess with my sisters all day long. I am here to play!" declared Baby Zo with a tricky look in her eye.

One bright morning, she decided it was time to wake everyone up. "Wakey, wakey!" she shouted. The twins groaned and cried, "Oh no, it's too early!"

"MOMMMMMMMM!"

they called for backup.

"Oh no, it's too early!"
"Wakey, wakey!"

The twins tried to brush Baby Zo away, hiding under their covers. But Baby Zo was undeterred. "Wakey, wakey!!" she insisted. "Here we go again," one of the twins whispered as they reluctantly got out of bed.

"Here we go again,"
"Wakey, wakey!"

Downstairs, they all headed to the kitchen for breakfast. "PANCAKES, PANCAKES, PANCAKES!" Baby Zo excitedly chanted. Mom, with a pointed finger, said, "Alright! First, you must sit and not make a mess." Baby Zo grinned and sat obediently in her highchair.

Steamy pancakes awaited her on the table, making her lick her lips in anticipation. But in a split second, FLUG! went the highchair straps, and PLOP went Baby Zo onto the tabletop.

"PANCAKES, PANCAKES, PANCAKES!"

The twins screamed, "NOOOOOO!" FLING! Up went the spoons and bowls. "MOMMMMMMM!" the twins cried out. As Mom stood there with her hand over her head, she thought to herself,

"Sister Blues, Terrible Twos."

"Sister Blues, Terrible Twos."
"mommmmmmm!"

Noon arrived, and Mom had an idea.
"Who wants ice cream?"
"Ice Cream! Ice Cream!" the twins said.
But Baby Zo had other plans. She
FLUNG
her arms, and the twins' ice cream went
flying into the air.

"Ice Cream! Ice Cream!"
"Ice Cream! Ice Cream!"

"**mommmmm!**" the twins yelled once more. Mom couldn't help but shake her head.

"Sister Blues. Terrible Twos. What are we going to do?"

"mommmmm!"
"mommmmm!"

Mom decided it was time for a change of surroundings and bundled the girls into the sticky car. As they drove off into the sunset, the twins plotted their next playtime move.

When the twins arrived at home they went into the playroom "CLUCK, CLUCK, CLUCK!" echoed as the twins bounced wooden blocks off the porcelain walls. Baby Zo woke up from her nap and charged towards the playroom. "Blockies!" she exclaimed.

The twins screamed in surprise, and a loud WHAM echoed as the wooden blocks collided. "MOMMMM!" cried the twins, again.

WHAM !
mommmm!

Mom, now with her hands on her hips, thought about what to do with Baby Zo's endless energy. Baby Zo covered her mouth and grinned, "I am cute as day. I MUST get my WAYYY."

As evening approached, dinner was served. Baby Zo sat in her highchair, giggling and giving herself a mashed potato bath. "Mashed potatoes are everywhere!" exclaimed Mom.
"Bath time!" she declared.

"Sister Blues, Terrible Twos."
"mommmmmm!"

The twins prepared for their bath, but Baby Zo had other plans. "SPLASH SPLASH!" Water went everywhere, and the twins realized Baby Zo was making a mess once again.

Baby Zo's energy was contagious, and the twins couldn't resist joining her for some splashy fun.

Baby Zo yawned, "I'm cute as day,
But this terrible two must head to bed."
So they all headed to bed,
ready for another day of
Sister Blues and Terrible Two's.